NATIONAL LAMPOON'S
Truly Tasteless
CARTOONS
THE BEST OF THE WORST

CB
CONTEMPORARY
BOOKS
CHICAGO

Library of Congress Cataloging-in-Publication Data

National lampoon's truly tasteless cartoons : the best of the worst.
        p.   cm.
     ISBN 0-8092-3913-2 (paper)
     1. American wit and humor, Pictorial.   2. National lampoon.
   I. National lampoon.   II. Title: Truly tasteless cartoons.
   NC1428.N376   1992
   741.5'973—dc20
                                                    92-24506
                                                       CIP

Cover illustration by Bud Grace
Back cover illustrations by Leo Cullum, Charles Rodrigues,
and Revilo.

These cartoons have previously appeared in regular and
special editions of *National Lampoon*® magazine.

Published by Contemporary Books, Inc.
Two Prudential Plaza, Chicago, Illinois 60601-6790
Manufactured in the United States of America
International Standard Book Number: 0-8092-3913-2

Cartoons By:

M. K. Brown

John Caldwell

Thomas W. Cheney

Bruce Cochran

Cotham

Leo Cullum

Bud Grace

Sam Gross

Tim Haggerty

John Jonik

Joe Kohl

Mankoff

Howard Margulies

Revilo

Charles Rodrigues

Brian Savage

P. Steiner

Ed Subitzky

Larry Trepel

P. C. Vey

Bill Woodman

Jack Ziegler

"Oh, Cecil, Cecil, Cecil . . . if only you'd read the instructions that came with your chain saw!"

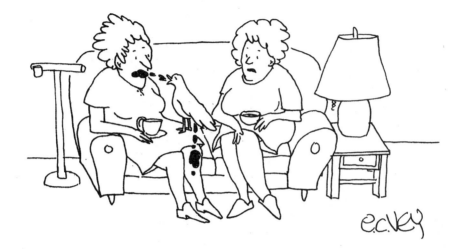

"Oh! He must be sick."

"Mr. Hallet, if we could put one of your hemorrhoids on this safety pin as bait, there's a good chance we could catch a fish."

"Wake up, Woofey! I have to make a good impression on this job interview!"

S.GROSS

"Yes, I can well imagine that it's not easy to whistle anymore, but give yourself time, Mr. Chase."

"More! Please, more! Oh, I've been such a naughty, handsome, enchanted prince!"

"I'm not hungry. I just want to look up her dress."

S GROSS

"Is he…dead?"

"It's a telegram from the governor.... 'Happy birthday to you.... Happy birthday to you.... Happy birthday, dear...'"

"Nice dog you got there, mister! Drop a quarter in the cup or else my monkey squeezes his balls."

"...Castration knife... castration knife... castration knife..."

"Sorry, no, but if you folks ever get up around Merton-Indiana way, you come by to supper with Mother and me."

"Et tu, Bruce?"

"I'll be frank with you, Charlene. I've used my body to get what I wanted."

A VISIT TO GRANDFATHER'S ALLIGATOR FARM

"Good evening. I've run out of gas. Would it be too much of an imposition for you and your lovely wife to step out into the street and push my car to a gas station?"

"Hey, Marlene, be a doll and stick this zucchini in your ass and show Ned your Jimmy Durante imitation."

"Don't lecture me on civil rights, Mr. Wilbur—you forfeited your civil rights when you came in my mouth down at the bus station."

"What's the matter, Lassie—is Timmy in trouble?"

"*The stitches can come out in seven or eight days, and I see no reason why you can't begin denying him sex in about two weeks.*"

"WHEELS? Fischer Bros. doesn't sell WHEELS!"

"Butchie's asleep, you should have no trouble with him. The first switch is the porch light. The one in the middle's for the living room, and this one will suck the face right off your skull. There's pizza in the fridge; we'll be home by eleven."

"It's not necessary to call Simmons in, Mr. Mount. I can take him out from here."

"Piss on me and you're dead."

S.GROSS

"There was an eighth dwarf, 'Lumpy,' but he died of cancer."

"We'll have to get a new bird, Mary. This one just isn't cleaning up the lice, dandruff, and dried skin the way it used to."

"Hello, boys, I'm Mister Rogers! Don't be frightened, I won't kill you."

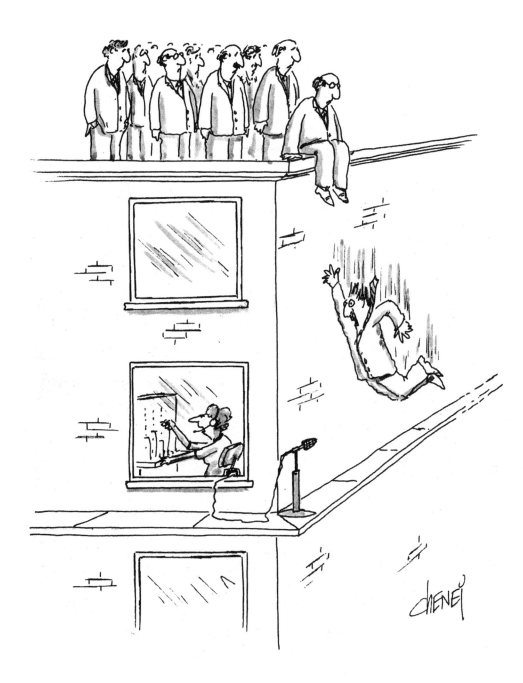

"At the tone, the time will be…"

"Good afternoon, sir. I'm Dr. Leonard Delray of Proctology Associates, Inc., down at the Busy Pilgrim Mall. As part of our Midsummer Wackiness Sale, we're giving door-to-door free estimates. So if you'll kindly bend over and spread them, we can start you on the road to affordable proctology service."

"We have to talk."

*"All right, all right—I'm sure you've all seen
somebody gettin' an enema before..."*

"Fongu!"

"You really took Muffy and Scott and Todd down to the lake and let them go...
honest? Have you got a note or something from them so I could be sure?"

"I said, 'Eat your fucking vegetables, you scum-sucking
pig.' What did you think I said?"

"Pass it on down the line: 'Anyone who plays with her tits will never see the promised land.'"

THE BIRTH OF A LEGEND

"Can I call you back, Ted? Half of my desk just exploded, some people are throwing shit at my window, and my secretary has been abusing her medication."

"Quick! Make fun of the size of his genitals and perhaps he'll retreat in embarrassment!"

"*Ticket, please.*"

"Pssst, c'mere . . . there's another peephole over here!"

"Maurice, show Irene and Joe the funny trick
you do with your colostomy bag."

"I'll give you five bucks if you let me sniff your cart."

S.GROSS

"Mama, get help! I jerked it right off!"

"And I tell you I searched desperately for a black elf! A Jewish elf! A female elf!
The only break I've gotten is that most elves are gay!"

S.GROSS

"Excuse me...the missus wants to know if you folks would like to stay for dinner."

"*I'm from the IRS. I'm afraid we've misused all your tax money. Could we have some more?*"

"Darling, we can't go on meeting like this. He's due to be wormed next week."

"Beatrice, over here! Peas the size of your brain! No exaggeration."

"You have only to glance at my wife's intimate undergarments and I shall be forced to kill you."

"I wouldn't say that jerking off ten times a day is a health risk, but maybe you should use your left hand once in a while."

"Don't take it so hard, Billy. I'm sure even professional ballplayers sometimes shit their pants when they're sliding into second."

"Is this it, Edward? Is this as kinky as we're going to get?"

"Did you know that 'getting fixed' means having your balls cut off?"

"Be careful! This soup is so hot, it's still bubbling!"

"*His prostate is just fine!*"

"Send Orgill in, will you? I have something I'd like to bounce off him."

"We are a very poor country, and we can't afford to buy electrodes for your testicles."

S.GROSS

"Don't pick those. Those are dingleberries."

"Herb, who did you say the doctor was who did your colostomy?"

"Oh, no! My best friend and my best friend's wife!"

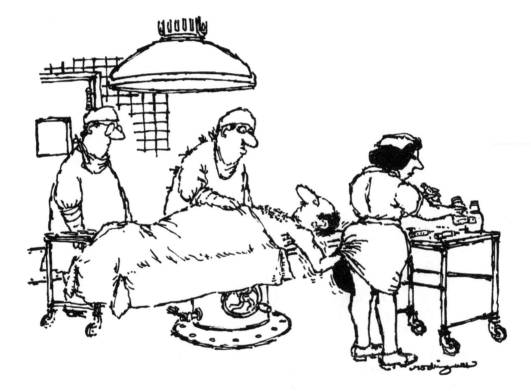

"Mr. Guzman, are you quite sure that you want to go through with this sex-change operation?"

*"Offhand I'd say you have an excellent case, Mr. Vogel.
How long ago was this autopsy performed on you?"*

"Do you have something for the control of premature ejac…ooo…ooo… ooooohhh…. Never mind."

"And while you're waiting for your order, don't forget to check out our free salad bar."

"Did anyone ever tell you you have body odor?"

"Wait! Come back! I don't even know your name!"

"*I left my wife this morning. Of course, it was only to go to work, but I feel good about it.*"

"*Do you get this joke, Harold? I don't. Do you understand this new humor, Harold? I don't. I just don't get it. Do you, Harold?*"